About the Author

Makenna Rooyakkers was born and raised in a small town in Southern Ontario, Canada. She writes about her experiences of life, and how everyone can learn to love themselves, no matter how hard. She is passionate about finding a creative outlet and hers is writing poetry and painting. As well as writing, she is an aspiring illustrator, who continues to follow her passions in the art world.

Letters of Love

Makenna Rooyakkers

Letters of Love

Olympia Publishers
London

www.olympiapublishers.com
OLYMPIA PAPERBACK EDITION

Copyright © Makenna Rooyakkers 2022

The right of Makenna Rooyakkers to be identified as author of this work has been asserted in accordance with sections 77 and 78 of the Copyright, Designs and Patents Act 1988.

All Rights Reserved

No reproduction, copy or transmission of this publication may be made without written permission.
No paragraph of this publication may be reproduced, copied or transmitted save with the written permission of the publisher, or in accordance with the provisions of the Copyright Act 1956 (as amended).

Any person who commits any unauthorised act in relation to this publication may be liable to criminal prosecution and civil claims for damage.

A CIP catalogue record for this title is available from the British Library.

ISBN: 978-1-80074-312-0

The works written in this book are purely the author's own thoughts and feelings, and do not reflect any person, or views to anyone related to the creation and publication of this book.

First Published in 2022

**Olympia Publishers
Tallis House
2 Tallis Street
London
EC4Y 0AB**

Printed in Great Britain

Acknowledgements

Acknowledgments to everyone whom I've grown up around, who I've ever met and have helped me put my feelings into words.

Poetry is an outlet when I can't say how I feel, and it has allowed me to translate my feelings to words on paper. Everyone who has been around me has supported me through everything despite my communication skills, or lack thereof.

Despite where I have moved some people have stuck with me while I have let others go, but that's just how things need to be sometimes. Those who have been here with me throughout everything, have been an inspiration for the things I write as well as the things I paint. I'm thankful for everyone who has come through my life, good or bad, as they have allowed me to be able to put my thoughts onto paper to share with others.

Section One
Finding Safety

Moon

I search the night skies

Skies full of the cold, wetness of winter's night,
Night time comes once again,
But this time I see her.
Her,
the light of the night,
She will always be found,
She will show you the way, She will take away your fear,
Fears of loneliness and death,
She will turn them into mysteries, Peace and happiness,
You are not alone,

She is always with you

Imperfection of Perfection

When I see you, I think to myself
How beautiful you are,

All the pain you've been through,
Has sculpted you,
You're carved with edges so rough and jagged
You are the imperfection of perfection

Emma

Alcohol runs through my blood to help contain my thoughts
As each day goes on

I reach again and again She's pulling me out of it My darkness and despair
My thoughts are no longer drowned away, But instead encapsulated by her mind
A tsunami of thoughts

Spills from my mouth to her ears She hears me
She saved me

Street Lights

Circles of light Lighting up the streets As I walk home
Bringing safety,
To my heart, mind, and soul,
They ease the pain
They ease the fear

That looms in the darkness It brings me home

Midnight Rain

Peaceful and calm,

Your pain is being washed away, Away with your thoughts,
The rain drops bring, A wave of serenity, Washing away
the old
Bringing alight the new, A feeling of awakening Brought
through
the midnight rain.

Serenity

She brings me home, Fills me with warmth,
She is the fireplace to my heart, Filling me with a burning passion She keeps me serene,
She is like the book you pick after years of forgetting,

She makes you remember all of her lessons once you open it up
You remember,

The peace

she has brought you.

Fire

He smells like a freshly lit campfire,
It is my new favourite scent
I seek to find it
The burning ashes, he leaves behind.
I see the burns, everywhere I go
Making my heart burn once more

I only wish to see the fires burn once more.

Section Two
The Pain You've Brought Me

Burning

Though I once loved

I felt I could not love again

Nor would I ever feel the love of another This feeling
 creates a hole so deep inside me It convinces me
I am unworthy

Nightmares

Being torn from who I thought to be To who I thought I was
Was a nightmare in itself Can I not be both?
Can I not listen to my heart and my mind? Why must I fight myself?
When neither is wrong nor right

Red Strings

No matter how thick or thin they don't care,
They will push it aside Despite what they hear The constant terror
That rushes through me

Keeps me from feeling the pain again, I know if I tell others
They'll blame it, On the red strings I wore that night

Shaken

From my past to my present

I stand confused on what comes next Hurt, battered and broken
With no truth being told I keep myself hidden Ashamed of the past
I feel disgusted

I don't know what comes next

Temptation

Each time I remember I feel like I'm on fire
To extinguish those memories Would be a dream come true
I always try

To drain away those memories, to make them forgotten.
The bottles are lining up
They are tearing me apart, I can't stop,
They give me a moment of happiness.

Section Three
Finding Myself Again

Memories

You will keep melting
 Turning into what they desire
 Do not forget
Remember

Do not let them terrorize you any more Take control

Fantasys

I know it's not real But I yearn for it
I reach for it

It's so far from my grasp

Reaching for it, pulls me far from reality It is my safe haven
Keeping me sane

Realities

I learn To grow.
To accept What's real,
What's fake.
I understand Reality
It guides me,

My fantasies were a dream, To protect,
They made me grow Now
I can accept My future.

Belonging

I feel true,

The lies are no longer spread I am honest
I feel no faults They listen
I speak

I feel wanted I belong

Travelling to my future

Every breath Is a reminder
 That I am here
I have lived.
I must continue. For I am,
The creator of my future.

Section 4
Loving All

Road Trips

Creating a life for oneself, a challenging feat
We must do our best
 Not just for ourselves
But for all those around us.
Our failures, Our mistakes, Our Successes
Are not only ours

But all those who stand by us.

Success

Through all the hardships I have fought
I have cried

So many waterfalls Oceans filled with pain, But here I am
In Front of it all

I admire all its beauty. Through pain
I have created a painting of detail That leads to the success of my life.

Free

I'm finally through I've found my own
Made peace with my thoughts,
Made a new home
I am proud Because
I am Free

Exploring

Newfound freedom Brings so much joy No more limits
I am no longer held back My fears push me
To pursue my dreams

They've brought endless possibilities I explore all my
passions
They show me a new home.

Differences of the Mind

Each thought

Shows us a new reality The process
Of thinking

Relies solely on you. Nobody is the same
We see another and compare

But never think what if they saw me Compare us to
themselves
And you will see

you are not who you think you are

Joyous Occasions

Discovered, or found a difference by word
That's what I thought when I met you You've melted my heart
You've shown me joy I accept your love
I give you mine

Our little encounters Have made for
Many joyous occasions.

Hard Patches

You make me cry,
You make me smile,
 I'm conflicted.
 Without your love
I would be lost Where should I go? Should I follow love
Or follow logic?
It is no simple topic

Your love is worth so much Could I ever let it go?

Butterflies

I've chosen

I will fly my emotions Keep on giving my love It is not worth losing For when our love meets It becomes a beautiful Colourful bliss.

Painting in Progress

When it falls

It looks as if the paint is flowing But I know the outcome
As a painting

Has a messy process As do relationships
The end is such a spectacle It gets refined
As energy flows in. Our love
Is a painting in progress.

www.ingramcontent.com/pod-product-compliance
Lightning Source LLC
LaVergne TN
LVHW041552060526
838200LV00037B/1248